BECOMING A WOUNDED HEALER

Becoming a Wounded Healer

CHARLES KISER

EW
EMPATHETIC WITNESS

CONTENTS

First Printing, 2025

CONTENTS

First Printing, 2025

To my colleagues. Your lives and spiritual care inspire me.

| 1 |

Introduction

In spring of 2024, Mallory Wyckoff and I cofounded The Healing Collective, a ministry that exists to create spaces for healing religious trauma. These spaces are meant to serve two distinct, and yet overlapping, groups of people. The first is survivors of religious trauma, and the second is faith leaders (in whatever form they come — pastors, elders, ministry leaders, spiritual directors, etc.). The overlap between the two groups exists because many of the latter group have also experienced religious harm themselves, and thus need to pursue their own healing work.

I am particularly interested in working with faith leaders. For starters, I am a faith leader. I was a church planter and pastor for sixteen years. I currently work with a network of faith leaders in the Post-Evangelical Collective. I have solidarity with faith leaders; I want the best for them. I want to share with them the tools and frameworks for trauma that have been transformative for me. Further, faith leaders are connected to a lot of people and care for a lot of people. In some ways, a focus on faith leaders is a strategic decision: walking alongside faith leaders not only hopefully helps them discover personal healing and wholeness, it also reduces harm and increases the possibility of healing and wholeness for the people in their spiritual care.

All of this raised a question for me at the outset of our work: *how do faith leaders become trauma-informed agents of healing?* I knew my own story and path, but I was curious to learn from others in hopes that their stories would inform our imagination about what offerings to create for other faith leaders wanting to take a similar journey.

So in fall of 2024, I interviewed fifteen pastors, therapists, and educators — seven women and eight men; including two queer colleagues and three colleagues of color — to ask them about their own journeys of becoming trauma-informed and trauma-responsive. As a matter of ethical research practice, I received the informed consent of interviewees to participate in this research, including their agreement to be quoted in writing. To protect their wellbeing and privacy, I use pseudonyms for all participants and alter identifying information as needed. I asked four primary questions:

1. What experiences have contributed to you becoming trauma-informed?
2. What are the most impactful learning environments related to trauma and healing that you have either participated in or facilitated? What made them impactful?
3. What do spiritual leaders need to become trauma-informed and a healing presence?

4. What would you like to see from a ministry focused on religious trauma awareness and healing?

After the interviews were complete, I poured over the 200+ pages and 80,000+ words of interview transcripts to look for themes, categories and concepts related to becoming trauma-informed. The stories were so inspiring, full of wisdom, and hopeful for what is possible and what could be. At the same time, it's an arduous process, and overwhelming at times to believe that so much data could be distilled into something compelling and useful. There was an aha! moment in my research where my eyes were opened to three major categories that surfaced in the interviews — and it made it worth all the work. Once I saw these themes in the stories, I started seeing them everywhere — in my own life and experience, and in my colleagues' lives more broadly.

Three Foundations of Trauma-Responsive Spiritual Care

In the remainder of this introduction, I'll share an overview of the three foundations of trauma-responsive spiritual care — that is, aspects of formation that contribute to someone becoming trauma-responsive. In chapters 2-5, I'll take a deeper look at each of the foundations with further nuance and quotes from the interviews.

I'm using the phrase "trauma-responsive" in distinction from "trauma-informed" because the end goal for our work is that faith leaders would be agents of healing, which includes knowing what trauma is but ultimately entails being able to respond constructively to it.

The three foundations are:

1. Trauma awareness
2. Pastoral skill development
3. Personal healing

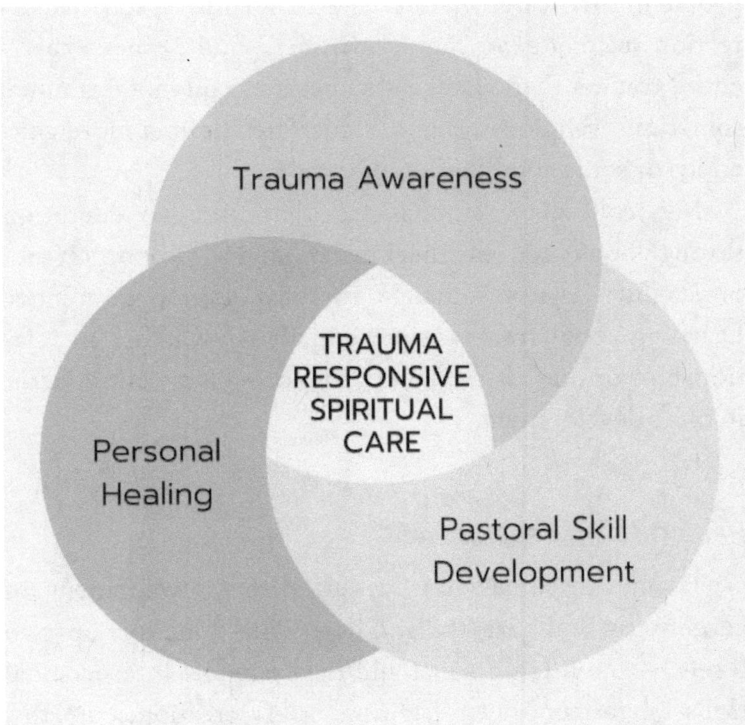

Trauma awareness

In order to become trauma-responsive one must become aware of trauma: what it is, how it functions in a person's brain and body, what it looks like off the page and in relationships. The leaders I interviewed became aware of trauma in three different ways: 1) they received education about trauma through books, classes, workshops, and conferences; 2) they encountered trauma through the stories of people in their care, whether church members, spiritual direction recipients, or family members; and 3) they experienced trauma themselves — sometimes childhood trauma, sometimes religious trauma, sometimes trauma more generally, or some combination of these.

My colleagues emphasized that trauma education through books and learning environments is important, but on its own is not sufficient to fully develop awareness. Learning about trauma experientially — whether in relationships or one's personal experience — is a critical factor in one's development.

Pastoral skill development

Trauma-responsiveness requires the development of certain pastoral care skills. These skills function on two levels — the interpersonal and the systemic. Interpersonal skills range from deep listening, safety creation, empathy, co-regulation, relational pace (slower is better), exercising power healthily, and knowing when to refer to trauma professionals (for those who are pastors but not therapists/doctors).

Systemic skills include cultivating and nurturing environments that are safe/brave/secure (there's a whole conversation about which words to use for this), teaching and leading groups in co-regulation and centering practices, assessing structures and systems for risk of harm, setting up institutional checks and boundaries, and curating worship and liturgy in ways that are sensitive to the trauma people carry into the room.

Personal healing

Perhaps the most resounding theme about becoming trauma-responsive is that it's not enough just to know about trauma, or even to be able to respond to it appropriately. Even the best intentions for being a healing presence can be hijacked by one's own wounds if they have not done their own personal work. Nearly all the leaders I spoke with agreed that we will invariably transmit our own pain to others if we do not process it and metabolize it.

I use the word *personal* and not "spiritual" or even "interior" because while personal processing includes those aspects, it extends beyond that to include one's body, in which the brain and nervous system exist, in which trauma is carried and either pent up or processed and discharged. Personal healing includes soul formation, emotional health, grieving loss, and also learning to pay attention to one's body to tend to where pain is being held. It means having an awareness of when one's nervous system becomes dysregulated and having the tools to return to calmness and settledness.

I hesitated initially to use the word *healing* because, for many, healing connotes a final state or reality, a place at which one arrives. And yet it is one of the words my colleagues used frequently to describe their own experiences. The truth they point to is that healing is a process, one we engage in our whole lives.

Leaders pursue personal healing in a variety of ways, including therapy, medical care, personal contemplative practice, spiritual direction, and the "healing village" of community.

Chicken or the Egg?

When I shared this research with a colleague she asked: is there a usual sequence for the three foundations? Does one foundation always come first or second or last? Does one begin, for instance, with awareness, and then move to pastoral skill development and then personal healing?

My colleagues agreed that personal healing is the deepest foundation of becoming truly trauma-responsive. And yet, when it comes to the process of how they became trauma-responsive, there were many paths. Some paths began with a personal shattering that required awareness of trauma and personal healing out of which grew the pastoral skills to care for others. Other paths began with hearing the stories of folks who were traumatized and seeking to understand their experiences. These stories required them to learn about trauma to understand what they were witnessing so they could care well for others. Only later did their learning surface their awareness of the harm and pain they had experienced themselves that required personal healing.

My own experience aligns with the latter trajectory. I first came into awareness of religious trauma by accident in a group of boarding game friends in my neighborhood (the stories of whom I tell in the book *Trauma-Informed Evangelism.*) I did not have the language to name what I was witnessing at the time, but I came to learn that it was experiences of spiritual abuse and religious trauma. This awareness helped me develop some necessary skills to care well for my friends and church folks, and in the course of that learning, I realized that part of my desire to care for these friends came from unresolved religious trauma that I was carrying myself. This led me to begin engaging in personal healing specific to my own religious trauma (and I'm still pursuing it — as one does).

Faith leaders can enter the on-ramps of formation with any of the foundations that interest them most. Some may be acutely wounded and need to pay attention first to personal healing. Others might want to care well for those they are walking alongside and so they might be initially more interested in trauma awareness and pastoral skill development. Trauma-responsive formation will eventually lead them more deeply into all three areas.

2

Cultivating Trauma Awareness

My colleagues cultivated trauma awareness through two different kinds of knowledge: theoretical and experiential. Theoretical knowledge relates to theories and intellectual frameworks. It's the kind of knowledge one gains from a book or a classroom lecture. Experiential knowledge is the knowledge gained through experience. It's what we learn through our relationships with other people and through our own lived reality. My colleagues learned about trauma secondarily through the experiences of others — their friends, family, clients, or parishioners — and also through their own direct, personal experience of trauma.

Before we explore how my colleagues learned about trauma, it seems fitting to describe what trauma is. I prefer two definitions. The first is from Bessel van der Kolk's popular book, *The Body Keeps the Score*. He defines trauma not as an adverse experience itself, but as the *imprint* of that adverse experience upon one's mind, brain, and body.[1] This imprint remains in one's body and, when activated, can manifest in any number of trauma responses, such as 'fight' (aggression), 'flight' (escape), 'fawn' (appeasement), or 'freeze' (dissociation).

Trauma can also be understood, according to Gabor Maté, not as the harmful thing that happened to us, but as "what we hold inside in the absence of an empathetic witness."[2] Trauma is fundamentally about disconnection. When our bodies feel powerless to defend themselves, when they get overwhelmed, and particularly, when there is no one near who is able to help us or at least be with us in the suffering, the pain of that harmful experience often becomes imprinted upon our nervous systems. If trauma is what we hold inside in the absence of an empathetic witness, then processing and healing trauma comes through the presence of an empathetic witness, someone who can bear witness to our pain, have compassion on us, and help us return to a sense of safety.

[Content warning: the following contains mention of spiritual abuse, sexual abuse, sexism, and heterosexism.]

Learning From Trauma Theory

My colleagues learned about trauma theory from a number of different sources. Some learned about it in seminary classes — others in counseling classes for a counseling degree program. Some completed extensive trauma certifications. Others attended workshops, conferences, or seminars where they expanded their knowledge base about trauma.

Mia, a pastor and theologian, mentioned that for her specifically it was books and podcasts that helped her build a theoretical awareness.

This theoretical awareness is important for faith leaders because, according to Tommy, a long-time pastor, "If you want to be a good pastor, you have to be trauma-informed. We know this now. If you don't understand how trauma works, you don't really know how to pastor people very well."

One way this awareness manifests is in learning a new language. The language of trauma names realities that were once hidden or misinterpreted as psychosis or character flaws. Which is why Ethan, an experienced pastor, would say, "You have to study, man. You have to understand the traumas that are out there and the sensitivities. And you need to be trained in language, trained in words, trained in posture...." It's the difference, for instance, in being able to notice that someone's hyper-aroused nervous system might be a trauma response that reflects a harmful past experience rather than a display of conviction and repentance over one's brokenness.

Trauma awareness relates to individual bodies — things like brain chemistry, nervous systems, and stress responses — as well as sources of harm and abuse inflicted upon those bodies. But trauma awareness also relates to the ways that systems and structures perpetuate trauma for individuals and even large groups of people (i.e., collective trauma). Harper, a trauma therapist, suggests that "spiritual leaders, especially those within any organized religion, need to understand the trauma that happens within that organization

as a structure, whether it's a history of patriarchal abuse or diminishing people who are marginalized...."

In *Trauma-Informed Evangelism* I described what Dr. Soong-Chan Rah calls "mediating narratives of supremacy," beliefs that elevate certain groups of people as superior (e.g., male, heterosexual, cisgender, and white) to other groups (e.g., female, queer, transgender/gender queer, black or indigenous people of color). Systems and structures are designed to privilege the "superior," more powerful group and disadvantage, and even traumatize, the "inferior," less powerful group.

These mediating narratives and the structures they shape require that trauma awareness includes becoming aware of one's social location in relation to power and marginalization. As Mia encourages, "Do the work to raise your consciousness...to be aware of the marginality that exists in a space....The things that were privileges for me kept me very unaware for a very long time until I had experiences that revealed my marginalization." Learning about trauma can, like Mia, show us areas where we have privilege and may reveal areas where we also experience marginalization.

Learning From Others' Trauma

When I asked Zane, a pastor and spiritual director, how he became trauma-informed, he said, "For me, probably more than anything is being a parent of a child that experiences disability. That kind of just opened the world for being a tad more trauma-sensitive. I would also say right along with that is being a spiritual director and hearing others people's stories of trauma. Particularly walking with women that have been on the outside of ministry [that is, women who have not been allowed to be ordained as ministers because of their church or denomination's theology and practice] and hearing their stories that are just so similar over and over and over about the different levels of rejection they have experienced."

Zane's initial trauma awareness came secondarily through the experiences of those he cared for — his child and female spiritual direction participants in particular. Hearing their stories, and witnessing firsthand his child's challenges with disability, "opened the world" for him.

My colleagues echoed this dynamic repeatedly: hearing stories of harm is a major pathway to trauma awareness. Lily, an experienced pastor, shared that her trauma awareness grew when she "started hearing story after story from the LGBTQ community about how the church had harmed them or rejected them or bait and switched them."

Aaron, a minister, activist, and trauma educator, has decades of experience walking alongside neighbors experiencing homelessness. He described the confusion he felt when his highly motivated neighbors struggled to find liberation: "I first started to try to understand why my neighbors had all of the desire to think differently, act differently, be different, then they were baptized, but things weren't shifting for them. They were still making impulsive decisions. They were still making decisions that frankly betrayed their own commitments, betrayed their own convictions, betrayed their own needs. And I didn't understand why. Then I stumbled upon trauma."

Trauma theory helped Aaron to understand the stories of his neighbors, what was happening in the bodies and brains of his traumatized neighbors who had been socially displaced and were living in survival mode. In this way, Aaron's experience reveals the interdependence of theoretical and experiential trauma awareness.

Ivy, like Aaron, Lily, and Zane, heard the stories of individual trauma within her congregation, but she also bore witness to the story of her congregation as a traumatized system. She described it as "seeing up close what it is like to be in a community that is operating with dysfunction — spiritual dysfunction, boundary dysfunction." Seeing the church as a body, the Body of Christ, alongside her growing awareness of trauma theory, helped her to see the ways her congregation had a "dysregulated nervous system, when your body is so dysregulated you are operating out of fear or reaction and not wholeness or health."

Learning From One's Own Trauma

My colleagues also learned about trauma by way of experiencing it directly themselves. I asked Rachel what experiences contributed to her becoming trauma-informed and she immediately responded: "My whole life." Several of my colleagues, like Rachel, experienced what are known as Adverse Childhood Experiences, or ACEs, which often create childhood trauma in those who live through them. ACEs include growing up in a violent family, experiencing food or housing insecurity, enduring verbal, mental, or sexual abuse, among other things.

In Rachel's case, some of her childhood trauma did not surface until she was an adult with children when her child's elementary school sought parents' consent to show a film on the topic of sexual abuse and protection from sexual predators. Rachel attended an advanced screening where the film shared a case study about an older man who lived next door to a family with a daughter. He groomed the daughter over time and preyed upon her.

After watching the film, Rachel walked home with a neighbor who lived nearby. The neighbor had a kid in the same class as Rachel's and asked if she was going to let her child watch the film. Rachel turned to her and said, "That was my story. That film happened to me." She quickly felt nauseated and felt her face turn "crimson red with shame" (both trauma responses). It was the first time she had ever mentioned it to anyone, and from that moment she began to learn more about abuse and trauma. Similar to Aaron's story, in which trauma studies helped him to interpret his friends' stories, the school film Rachel watched helped her to recognize the abuse and trauma in her own story.

For other colleagues, therapy was an educational process where they were able to reflect on their experiences in light of the information and guidance they received from their trauma-informed therapists.

While some colleagues learned about trauma through experiences of childhood trauma, others learned about it through traumatic experiences in adulthood, particularly experiences of religious abuse and trauma. Lena, for instance, experienced a personal “shattering” after being spiritually abused when she was in a church leadership position. Reflecting on that story, she said, “My own trauma work is what opened me up to being trauma-informed and I think what opened up my own trauma work was seeing injustices and inconsistencies within church leadership structures where the way church leaders behaved and decisions they made didn’t align with their values and caused harm to people. One of those situations led to my own shattering, which kind of forced me to do my own trauma work.”

> "Therapeutically shallow pastors are just waiting to transmit their pain onto other people because they haven’t processed it." - Tommy, pastor and survivor

Tommy experienced religious abuse and trauma in his church work and also witnessed it in the life of his queer child who was rejected by the church. Trauma therapy gave him an education about what was happening in his body and brain and helped him to process the pain he was carrying. It was so impactful for him that he frequently encourages other pastors to go to therapy too: “I’m telling pastors all the time, if you don’t have a therapist, what are you waiting on? It’s not because you’re all screwed up. You need to be educated. Find somebody to help you because that’s the moment we’re in. Therapeutically shallow pastors are just waiting to transmit their pain onto other people because they haven't processed it."

Actions for Cultivating Awareness

If you're interested in beginning or continuing to cultivate your own trauma awareness, my colleagues offer several suggestions for where to start. Consider engaging one of these that interests you:

1. Learn from a resource about trauma — it could be a book, article, video, or podcast. You can find a list of recommended resources at the end of this book.
2. Ask permission to hear someone's story about their own adverse experiences — a parishioner, family member, or neighbor — and reflect on it in light of a trauma resource you're learning from. When someone graces you with a story, take care not to fix, advise, or correct them, but simply to listen. Ask questions out of your curiosity. Thank them for trusting you enough to share.
3. Connect with a trauma-informed therapist or spiritual director (not all are trauma-informed) and share your story with them. If you're not sure how to find a trauma therapist, consider using a resource like www.psychologytoday.com and filter your search by choosing therapy types like "trauma-focused," "EMDR" (a specific trauma therapy that helps to integrate traumatic memories through rapid eye move-

ments), and "somatic" or "somatic experiencing." "Attachment-based," "cognitive-behavioral therapy (CBT)," and "Internal Family Systems (IFS)," are also helpful types of talk therapy through which you could address trauma experiences. Raise your awareness through what you learn about yourself in the process. Through such work you'll also simultaneously engage one of the other foundations of trauma-responsive formation: personal healing.

| 3 |

Offering Trauma-Responsive Care

If trauma awareness is learning the language and concepts of trauma, then pastoral skill is learning how to apply that knowledge responsibly in one's spiritual care for others.

Trauma awareness also includes the acknowledgment of both individual and systemic dynamics. Trauma appears in individual bodies and brains, but it also exists and is perpetuated within people groups, systems, and structures. People groups can experience trauma together, called collective trauma (e.g., Covid was a global experience of collective trauma). Systems and structures built to advantage certain powerful groups of people (e.g., white, male, heterosexual, cisgender) to the neglect or oppression of less powerful groups (e.g., people of color, female, queer, transgender) can perpetuate the potential for trauma in groups on the downside of the power difference.

Faith leaders who want to care well for those who carry trauma must likewise tend to both the individual and systemic aspects of trauma. They need skills to offer helpful pastoral care to traumatized individuals who seek them out; and they need leadership skills to cultivate a trauma-sensitive environment in the collective and structural expressions of their congregations.

My colleagues shared their perspectives on both interpersonal and systemic pastoral skills for responding to trauma. They had so much to offer that I must err on the side of brevity to give you a sense of the scope of their imagination. This chapter will focus on interpersonal skills; the next chapter will focus on systemic skills. While the scope of skills they suggest is broad, neither they nor I intend this to be a comprehensive list. That trauma-responsive pastoral skills exist beyond this collection indicates just how wide and far-reaching is the impact of trauma and need for healing.

Interpersonal Skills

At the heart of all these interpersonal skills is a commitment first to do no harm to those who have already been harmed. As James, a trauma educator and professional, said, "in some ways, trauma-informed is a posture of not making things worse." Trauma-responsive skills are as much about knowing one's limits and role as they are about constructive relational interventions.

1. Holding Space

Several colleagues used the phrase "holding space," to describe the ability to make room for the pain of another and to bear witness to it without projecting one's own anxiety on to the survivor. Lily, an experienced pastor, suggested that spiritual leaders "need to be comfortable with what they don't know and an awareness that it's not their job to heal the trauma, it's their job to hold space for the impact of that trauma and to walk with the person experiencing it." James agreed: "Resist the urge to try and fix it." Releasing the need to advise, fix, or save a trauma survivor helps to create the space necessary for offering healthy spiritual care.

"It's not [your] job to heal the trauma, it's [your] job to hold space for the impact of that trauma and to walk with the person experiencing it." - Lily, pastor

Holding space is also about monitoring and regulating one's own internal responses so that they are not projected upon survivors in potentially harmful ways. Harper, a trauma therapist, describes how "we go alongside [survivors] to be very, very truthful about what happened without minimizing it or being nice, putting it under the rug, or talking about forgiveness way too soon — the things we say when our own anxiety drives these solutions that are not healing but instead perpetuate greater harm."

2. Body Care

Trauma-responsive faith leaders see the extent to which trauma impacts the body and seek to help others' care for their bodies as an expression of pastoral care. James suggests that "there are small things that people can do that don't require expertise to make a big difference...oftentimes nutrition and hydration get neglected because it's just chaotic, right?" Trauma-responsive care might entail something as simple offering someone water or a snack. It might also entail suggesting physical movement — going on a walk, practicing yoga, or getting a massage — as a way of discharging traumatic energy from survivors' bodies. One practice suggested by *Strategies of Trauma Awareness and Resilience* is called "Shake it off," in which individuals shake, in sequence, their left hand, right hand, left leg, and then right leg in cycles of eight, six, four, two, and one repetitions. Participants are encouraged to count the number of repetitions out loud because it helps to bring back online the executive function of the brain's prefrontal cortex.

3. Slow Pace

Zane, a pastor and spiritual director, observed that "when you're going fast, you inflict trauma on people because anger is a fast-moving emotion. So much trauma comes from anger. Speed demands control...and so slowing down allows us to listen." Faith leaders who cultivate a slower ministry (and internal) pace are both less likely to inflict trauma on others in their haste and hurry — states which activate one's nervous system into fight or flight responses — and more likely to have the capacity to hold space, listen, and hear deeply the stories and hurts of those in their care.

4. Deep Listening

"Until we learn to listen, we're just going to keep inflicting trauma on people," Zane said. Listening well — hearing stories of harm and learning about people's experiences of abuse and trauma — is a transformative practice both for faith leaders and for those who are able to share their story with a deep listener. It creates context and sensitivity for faith leaders. And it provides an empathetic witness for survivors' stories that contributes to their healing and recovery from trauma.

Mia, a pastor, when asked what spiritual leaders need to become trauma-informed, immediately responded with, "The ability to listen, learning how to listen, learning how to manage one's own parts." Similar to Harper's comments about holding space and listening, "managing one's own parts" requires that people are aware enough of the dynamics and wounds in their own interior that they are not projected upon, transferred to, or centered instead of the survivor and their story.

Victor, a pastor, honed in on one particular interior dynamic for faith leaders that stems from their investment in the structures and systems of the church. When people complain, faith leaders are naturally put on the defensive, and find themselves defending decisions, structures, and institutions. This defensive posture is at odds with a listening posture. "We need to have a practicing community," Victor suggested, "where we can learn to listen and not be defensive."

5. Expressing Belief

Trauma-responsive faith leaders believe the stories that survivors share with them. As empathetic witnesses, they come alongside those who have suffered harm as allies, to stand against the abuse and injustice that occurred, to name it as such, and to grieve the pain and loss with the survivor. In Zane's words, this means "believing what people say about their own experience, not interpreting their experience through our experience, but believing what they say, knowing that the only person that can understand what it's like from an internal perspective is the person describing it."

6. Keeping Boundaries

Faith leaders who care well for those with trauma practice healthy boundaries. They are not always available or on call. This creates space for their own processing and recovery, and also resists unhealthy enmeshed or codependent relational dynamics with survivors. To recall James's comments, trauma-responsive faith leaders are not the saviors or fixers and thus are released of the responsibility to be everything survivors need. Lily advised that faith leaders need "really healthy boundaries — because people who have trauma sometimes don't keep strong boundaries for themselves. Sometimes your job as a healer is to be boundaried for both of you."

7. Repair

Faith leaders will make mistakes, even with the best of intentions. They may even sometimes be complicit in the harm and trauma they are seeking to heal. Part of being a trauma-informed leader, Mia shared, is "letting go of this idea that we're going to be perfect or that we're not going to make mistakes, and moving to this posture of 'I'm probably going to say something wrong, do something wrong, do something that's triggering for someone, and my role then is to just be able to hold space for someone reflecting their experience back to me.'" Faith leaders pursue repair with people in their congregations using the same skills necessary for trauma-responsive care, like holding space, listening, and owning their mistakes with humility.

8. Refer and Resource

Trauma-responsive faith leaders know their limits. If they are not trained trauma professionals, faith leaders have the skill to recognize when someone needs a referral for care that the faith leader is not qualified to offer. Lucas and Harper, both trauma therapists, agreed that a good indication for referral is when individuals are experiencing ongoing biological symptoms, including nightmares, social anxiety, insomnia, or difficulty functioning. Lily, an experienced pastor, also suggested that in addition to referral to a trauma therapist, faith leaders can share trauma awareness resources with survivors who reach out for help to give them frameworks for understanding what is happening in their bodies and tools for calming their nervous systems.

This is not to say that faith leaders do not have a role as a healing presence in survivor's lives. Sophia, a ministry leader and trauma recovery coach, was keen to caution pastors not to "take the easy way out" in referring people to therapy without any other engagement. Therapy is needed, for sure, and at the same time "people really need spiritual leaders and spiritual spaces."

4

Leading Trauma-Responsive Communities

Interpersonal skills for responding to trauma within faith communities are insufficient on their own because trauma and harm also have systemic and structural aspects. As I mentioned in the last chapter:

> *Trauma appears in individual bodies and brains, but it also exists and is perpetuated within people groups, systems, and structures. People groups can experience trauma together, which is known as collective trauma (e.g., Covid was a global experience of collective trauma). Systems and structures built to advantage certain powerful groups of people (e.g., white, male, heterosexual, cisgender) to the neglect or oppression of less powerful groups (e.g., people of color, female, gay, transgender) can perpetuate the potential for trauma in the less powerful groups of people.*

Pastors need certain systemic skills, therefore, in addition to interpersonal skills, to lead their congregations with a trauma-responsive posture.

Aaron and his trauma training organization go to great lengths to understand the cultures of the organizations and churches they partner with. His organization engages in culture learning and in-depth interviews with key stakeholders as a condition for training people in trauma-responsive care. Aaron's rationale is rooted in the systemic nature of trauma: "Because it's cultures. It's not just people."

Ivy, a ministry leader, suggested that "trauma-informed care can really be a framework or a tool for how to set up community for changing times in the West," imagining that such a framework could potentially change everything, such as where a church meets, its rhythms for gathering, how ministries are named, the type of music, the length of services, or what voices are incorporated and centered.

Here are some of the systemic skills — not intended as a comprehensive list, but rather a starting point — that my colleagues shared for nurturing trauma-responsive faith spaces.

Systemic Skills

1. Cultivating Safe/Brave Spaces

Pastors cultivate safety interpersonally as they hold space for others, listen deeply, and believe the stories they are told. This sense of safety is also needed on a collective level within the church when it gathers. Lucas, a trauma therapist and former pastor, said: "If there's one thing that I would say matters it's that the priority would be on safety creation. Every human that walks in is struggling to feel safe."

Lucas shared an example of what safety creation might look like. He referenced the popular worship song, "Good, Good Father." While it was a really meaningful song for many, Lucas observed, roughly half of any given congregation likely did not experience having a good biological father, and might feel like they are "betraying themselves to sing those words and try to even imagine God in that context." Lucas suggested that a pastor seeking to create a sense of safety might say, "Hey, if this is not your experience, I get it. I'm sorry. That's not what you deserve. And so if you don't want to sing this, don't."

Creating safety involves acknowledging the pain that people carry and then inviting their agency in deciding how they will or will not participate. Honoring the agency of others, through informed consent and invitations to opt-in/out, is an important part of safety creation for survivors, particularly because abuse and trauma robbed them of agency.

Aaron, however, sees problems with the language of safety: "The minute you put five people in a room, you've probably got an unquantifiable number of triggers and activations possible. That's why I don't believe in safety.... I chose not to use that word years ago, because I think many people believe that safe means no activation, safe means no hurt." Aaron prefers to speak instead of security: "Security as a word offers a more robust frame of reconciliation and restoration for me."

Similarly, Lena said: "I don't think, as leaders or pastors, we can completely avoid triggering trauma or triggering people. And so I actually think there's a deeper sense of the goal of how we want to cultivate brave space when stuff comes up or where there's some intensity warnings...I think trying to avoid [triggering people] is actually unhelpful."

Lena believes in the importance of acknowledging the pain in a room with trigger or 'intensity' warnings, but at the same time believes that triggering people is unavoidable. If we sought to anticipate and acknowledge every possible trigger we might run out of space to do anything else. Cultivating safety — or security, or brave space — therefore does not mean the absence of triggers or nervous system activation in a church environment, but rather that the pain that is triggered is acknowledged and compassionately witnessed, and that survivors are supported to exercise their agency to care for themselves and tend to what surfaces in whatever ways are best for them. The goal of a brave space is for people to have the safety to process their dysregulation and move through difficult experiences in community.

I helped to facilitate a gathering recently with faith leaders around racial awareness and justice. We heard stories and watched videos of injustice and oppression, particularly the testimony of a husband whose wife, a Black woman, died after childbirth because her doctors did not listen to her cries for help. I could feel my own nervous system activating because of the heaviness of the story, and I could sense tension and dysregulation in the room as well. Avoiding that activation and dysregulation would actually not be helpful to our goal of racial awareness and justice. We needed instead to be able to experience the pain, learn from it, and process it so it didn't remain in our bodies. And so after listening to these stories, we participated in a body movement exercise together to release any painful energy from our bodies. This is but one example of what a brave/safe space might look like.

In some ways safety cultivation is a frame for all the systemic skills to follow — all of them contribute to creating spiritually safe and healing environments for those who participate.

2. Releasing and Sharing Power

Zane, a pastor and spiritual director, observed that positions of power can have negative effects on people's personalities. Because of the way power can corrupt, Zane concluded, "I really think a constant reminder for moving into those positions [of power], especially in faith communities and church communities, is divestment of power. It should be a divestment of power rather than a gathering of power. You should consistently be looking for ways not to get your way instead of looking for ways to force your way through."

Divestment of power means that decisions are made within the community that pastors or senior leaders do not control or manage, and that other leaders are entrusted to make decisions that align with the community's values. Divestment of power means that every leader or person of power in a community is subject to the feedback and accountability of other leaders. Divestment of power means that no single person or small group of people has unilateral authority within a community, but are rather open and subject to the input of the broader community. Divestment of power means that a leader's posture with others is "power with" others and God rather than "power over" others.

In *Trauma-Informed Evangelism*, one of the ways I defined abuse was the harm done in the context of a power differential, where one person or group has more power and another person or group has less power. Substantial power differentials within a faith community create the conditions in which spiritual abuse and trauma can occur. One of the ways to subvert this dynamic, as Zane suggested, is to distribute power broadly within the system, minimize power differentials as much as possible, and establish accountability and checks for those in the positions of greatest power. This divestment of power mitigates its corrupting influence and contributes to the cultivation of safety within the community.

3. Engaging Ethnography

If deep listening is an interpersonal trauma-responsive skill, then its systemic sibling is ethnography. Ethnography, drawn from the fields of sociology and anthropology, is the practice of listening deeply to a culture or system and then reflecting on the sum of what is heard for the sake of learning, understanding, and discerning. It includes the practices of participant observation (experiencing a particular culture or community for oneself), interviewing cultural informants, analyzing interview data, and writing a summary of the themes that emerge from observation and interviewing.

"I think pastors should learn ethnography," Aaron advised. "I know that doesn't sound like it has much to do with trauma, but it's the posture of listening that it requires, right? It's tending to a culture as a participant observer. I would say ethnography as a pastoral practice would be critical because I think those are the tools spiritual leaders need in order to know how to be with people without trying to take over and fix."

Ethnographic practice has many benefits for trauma-responsive care. Aaron identified it as an alternative to "taking over" and "fixing" — or, in Zane's words, "gathering power." Ethnography is a form of divesting or releasing power over people and instead coming alongside of them to listen for the way forward. Ethnography helps pastors understand their context so that they can account for and acknowledge the pain a community is carrying, an important part of safety creation. Pastors who listen deeply to their communities learn the stories of abuse and trauma, the pain points, the triggers. This knowledge informs their cultivation of safety as they lead worship, preach, teach, and care for the congregation.

4. Facilitating Embodied Spiritual Practices

In the same way ethnography and deep listening are systemic and interpersonal sides of the same coin, embodied spiritual practices are what the interpersonal skill "body care" looks like in communal form. Embodied spiritual practices are ways that spiritual community members engage and attune to their bodies in the context of prayer or worship — whether through breathing, body scans, postures for prayer, or identifying emotional sensations in one's body. "I think embodied spiritual practices are very missing in the church," Lena reflected.

Embodiment, or "coming home to our bodies," as Lena phrased it, is important for trauma-responsive work because trauma disconnects us from our bodies. We might dissociate from our pain, or seek to numb it with substances or screens, rather than attuning to it within our bodies and allowing it to work its way through us and metabolize.

Lena leads listeners in embodied spiritual practices when she preaches: "I preached last week and invited people as I was reading the text to listen with their body. What do you see? What do you hear? What do you smell? What do you taste? What are the things that come alive for you? We need practices that help us learn how to live in our bodies and be attentive to them."

5. Establishing Structures of Support

Not every environment within a spiritual community is appropriate for survivors to share their stories and receive the care that they need. My pastoral colleagues reflected on ways they sought to develop structures of support for those who were deeply wounded. Victor, for instance, mentioned the need for "triage" when people come to talk about their experiences of abuse and trauma in his work as a pastor, which for him amounted to offering the survivor someone to talk to (a pastoral intake of sorts and initial care), trauma resources, and connection to a therapist if needed. This triage structure is the systemic side of the "refer and resource" interpersonal skill to the extent that there may be a defined process within a congregational system for walking with those who seek out spiritual care for trauma.

Victor also realized the need for more substantive care than triage, particularly for those with experiences of religious trauma. So he helped to develop a six-week support group that he co-leads, as a pastor, alongside two therapists who were also members of the church. In this support group, survivors were educated in the concepts of abuse and trauma, invited to share their stories as they were willing, and then referred to therapists if they desired to do further processing after the group concluded.

6. Equipping Others in Trauma-Responsive Care

My colleagues suggested that pastors should not be the only ones within a church who know how to respond well to trauma. Ministry leaders, church staffs, and indeed, the entire church benefits from training in trauma-responsive care.

Victor shared one way he equips his ministry team to respond with deep listening instead of with defensiveness: "Before you respond to anyone's complaint, ask three questions. It gets you in a listening posture: 'Tell me more about that.' 'What exactly are you upset about?' 'Okay, where did the communication break down?' Don't make a comment

until you ask those three questions, seek to understand before being understood."

> "How are we educating, forming, and engaging the hearts of people so they have a broader imagination, too? I think there's a subversive way to handle pain in the room that helps equip everyone." - Lena, pastor

Lena wondered, "How are we educating, forming, and engaging the hearts of people so they have a broader imagination, too? I think there's a subversive way to handle pain in the room that helps equip everyone, rather than just trying to avoid it, but instead offering compassionate presence." Embodied spiritual practices, for instance, are a way both to help participants to attune to their bodies, and simultaneously a way to educate them about the body and trauma that helps them care well for others. When a preacher extends empathy and compassion for a survivor of trauma in a story within their sermon, they model for the congregation this same empathetic witness for their own lives. When the worship leader acknowledges the pain in the room that might make it difficult to sing particular songs, it equips others with eyes to see pain in the room that they may not carry themselves.

7. Assessing Systems and Structures

Trauma-responsive leaders, in their efforts to cultivate brave spiritual spaces, need to be able to assess the health and equity of systems and structures within their churches to lower the risk of harm. For instance, Mia, a pastor, critiqued church systems with rigid hierarchical structures of power as susceptible to abuse and trauma.

Rachel, a pastor and theologian, shared her own experience of being a woman in a position of power within an institution and being subjected to harassment and bullying "from below" — from those with whom she had positional authority, but because of her gender, did not have relational authority. "There's nothing out there to help people deal with that," she said. "Part of the solution is we have to take down patriarchy, not to replace it with matriarchy, but to take it down and examine it and interrogate it and say, okay, how is this related to all these harms for everybody?"

Ivy recounted a church staff she was a part of that had an unhealthy and dysregulated church culture. An interim minister came in and listened deeply to the church and staff and their input revealed "a lot of things they wanted to hide, like unhealthy church culture, patriarchal forms of leadership, hierarchical forms of leadership, LGBTQ+ and the question of affirming or not affirming."

Faith leaders most naturally assess systems and structures in their communities through their ethnographic practice and as they listen to the experiences of leaders and congregants. Because faith leaders are often so immersed in their own congregational contexts, it can sometimes be helpful to invite the outside perspective of coaches or consultants, as Ivy's church did, who can engage the same kind of ethnographic practice that faith leaders would use to listen deeply to their community and then offer their assessment.

8. Nurturing Healthy Theological Imagination

Aaron noted the role of meaning making in trauma healing and resilience. How a survivor interprets and makes meaning of their experiences has a strong connection to whether the harm they experience becomes trauma in their body, or whether they are able to experience growth and resilience through the harmful experience instead.

A significant element of meaning making is theological or spiritual imagination. How we understand and imagine God and ourselves impacts both how we respond to potentially traumatic experiences and the degree to which we either resist or become complicit in potentially traumatic experiences for others. Lena offered an example, describing "the old system of fear and shame and behavior modification," and how "it forces some inner disconnection when your grounding center is a place of total depravity and you're wrong [in your essence]. It's actually really uncomfortable to think about living inside of a body." She suggested countering this imagination with a sense of humanity's "original goodness," which would free people to connect and attune to their bodies without a sense of shame or self-loathing.

Trauma-responsive leaders nurture healthy theological imagination in their preaching, teaching, and spiritual care that resists violent, abusive, or shaming imagination about God or self and instead emphasizes belovedness, goodness, justice, and healing.

Inner Work Required

As important as these pastoral skills are, my colleagues consistently noted that skill development does not go deep enough. Unless leaders tend to their own pain, attune to the trauma in their own bodies, and pursue soul formation for themselves, their pain and wounds will ultimately hijack their best attempts to be trauma-responsive. Tommy, a veteran pastor and trauma survivor, put it this way: "Therapeutically shallow pastors are just waiting to transmit their pain onto other people because they haven't processed it." In the next chapter, we'll turn to the final, and perhaps most important, foundation of trauma-responsive formation: personal healing.

| 5 |

Pursuing Personal Healing

My colleagues consistently emphasized the foundational role that personal healing plays in becoming trauma-responsive.

Ethan, a pastor, recounted a time when he promoted a recovery program during his church's Sunday service. After the service, a "super raw guy" in the recovery program approached him and asked, "Hey, man. You ever do a step study before?" Ethan said no. The guy replied: "Well how the hell can you be up there speaking about that shit if you've never done it yourself?"

Ethan then shared why he told the story: "The reason I bring that up is because the best way for leaders to be trauma-informed is to actually deal with your own trauma and to really become transparent and real. What we noticed was very few pastors who would do that."

Harper, a trauma therapist, shared a similar sentiment. When she was asked what spiritual leaders need to become trauma-informed and a healing presence, her immediate response was: "Spiritual leaders really need to do their own work. They need to examine their history and do their therapy. They need to do the thing that they want other people to do. That's paramount."

> "Spiritual leaders need to do their own work. They need to do the thing that they want other people to do." —Harper, trauma therapist

It's not sufficient just to learn about trauma intellectually. Cultivating trauma awareness is part of becoming trauma-responsive, but falls short on its own. Wounds are not ultimately healed through knowledge acquisition. "You can't just do three training sessions, and call it a day and say you're ready to go," Victor, a pastor, said. "People are really going to have to come to grips with their own trauma."

Lena, an experienced pastor, agreed that leaders need more than just good education about trauma. "I have read that just doing trauma-informed training doesn't really do anything to change how people show up in trauma-informed ways in their context. Actually, leaders doing their own trauma work changes how they show up in trauma-informed ways in their context or in their conversation....I think there's a chasm of separation between intellectualizing information and understanding the emotional, embodied experience of how harm impacts somebody."

The stakes are high for faith leaders' own healing, especially because they may transmit their own unhealed wounds and pain onto those to whom they offer spiritual care. Faith leaders need to "come to a least a little place of healing," Victor suggested, "because if they're not healed, then they're going to bleed all over everybody and they're going to make it about themselves."

Similarly, Lena observed that our wounds can become poison, where "we live from a place of reactivity and we vomit that poison all over.... We are either unleashing vitriol and releasing poison...or we're tending to [our wounds], and I think they actually release healing and medicine to the world. We're showing up with medicine, healing those things that are broken. We're either adding to the brokenness of the world and the pain and reactivity, or we're unleashing healing and wisdom from those very same things."

My colleagues were careful not to define healing as a destination at which one arrives or a task which one completes. Ivy, a ministry leader, said, "healing is not a linear path" but a process that requires space and time. Lena described healing as "a way of living." When Victor spoke of his own healing journey, he said, "I don't know any other way except for time and consistency. I needed those ten years with [my therapist] and I'm still going through counseling."

Pastoral Skill Requires Personal Healing

Faith leaders' personal healing is not only important for harm reduction — so that leaders will harm fewer people out of their own pain — but also because it is foundational to being a trauma-responsive agent of healing. Faith leaders will only be able to develop competency in trauma-responsive pastoral skills to the extent that they have engaged the interior work that sustains it.

Oliver, a pastor, imagined his own role as a pastor in relation to trauma therapists and the interior work needed to both create safe places (i.e., a systemic skill) and to be a safe place for people (i.e., an interpersonal skill): "What's my job? It's creating safe places for people and even beyond that, being a safe place for people and doing some of my own work so I'm not freaking triggered all the time and then reacting and then triggering them. Being a more non-anxious presence."

Harper pointed out that bearing witness to deep pain and suffering can cause anxiety to surface for those who observe it. If that anxiety is not addressed outside of that pastoral moment, it will inevitably be projected — unhelpfully at best, harmfully at worst — onto survivors: "When I'm with somebody who's in great pain and experienced great injustice, being very present to them in that degree of agony is challenging. The degree to which we're with our own pain is the degree to which we can be with another's. This is so significant because our anxiety, our fear of our helplessness just wants us to come up with something [instead of being present and listening]."

Mia, a pastor, described how contemplative practice helped her engage the interior work so that she could hold space well for others: "One of the things that's really important about contemplative practice is it allows us to find some sense of internal spaciousness from which we can have a choice whether to react or not."

Tommy observed that his own participation in therapy made him a better pastor. It strengthened his ability to empathize and grew his understanding of how trauma works: "My capacity for empathy, my empathic imagination, was deeply expanded by my own therapeutic journey, which then lends itself to a deeper understanding of people when they come to you. You have a new set of glasses where you can see things you just could not see before."

Pathways to Healing

How did my colleagues find personal healing? What did they do to participate in God's healing work within themselves? They identified four main pathways by which they pursued their healing journeys: 1) therapy; 2) spiritual direction; 3) contemplative practice; and 4) healing villages. Most engaged some combination of these four, but not all of them. These pathways are not intended to represent an exhaustive list of pathways, simply the ones mentioned most often by my colleagues.

1. Therapy

"What would I tell my younger self?" asked Tommy, a longtime pastor. His answer: "Get a therapist." "People need to be in therapy," Rachel, a pastor and theologian, asserted. "They somehow need to work on their own business, especially those who are carrying significant trauma. A lot of people going into the helping professions do so because they're carrying trauma." Lily, a skilled pastor, added that therapy is important for faith leaders because it provides "a place to put the things you're carrying," pointing to the secondary stress and trauma that faith leaders often experience by virtue of bearing witness to the pain of others.

Therapy can include talk therapy, which can help individuals examine their personal histories, family of origin dynamics, attachment styles, and internal dialogue (e.g., through Internal Family Systems theory). Because trauma lives in the body, often inaccessible to the rational part of one's brain, talk therapy alone is insufficient for processing trauma. Trauma therapy engages body and brain-based practices like EMDR (rapid eye movement that helps integrate traumatic memories) or somatic experiencing (recalling traumatic memories while attending to their impact on one's body).

2. Spiritual Direction

My colleagues also participate in spiritual direction as part of their personal healing process. Ivy described spiritual direction as "a space to comfortably and in a secure and safe environment be able to process what's going on, how it's connected spiritually, and what God is doing." She started her healing journey with trauma therapy, and then transitioned to spiritual direction after she gained the tools she needed. She saw a benefit to this progression: "I really do think that to get to a point where I can see a bigger and more expansive God, I had to understand myself."

I was struck by similar dynamics between talk therapy and spiritual direction in the experiences of several of my colleagues. Oliver, for instance, shared about how in spiritual direction, "I could look deeply into my feelings and my history and why I do the things I do and why I'm all worked up and how things played out in my own life."

Mia started working with a spiritual director who introduced her to Internal Family Systems (IFS), a prominent therapeutic framework. Whereas Ivy started with therapy and moved to spiritual direction, Mia's spiritual direction led her to seek out a trauma therapist with more expertise in IFS and somatic experiencing. People have different needs and journeys as they heal.

Tommy, a former pastor and spiritual director, sensed that spiritual direction might be a good first step for many pastors: "It seems to me that spiritual direction is more accessible for pastors who have not yet started a good therapy journey. They'll do that before they'll do therapy, because therapy sounds like 'I've got to fix something' to people who don't know. And spiritual direction sounds like 'I'm doing something spiritual to enhance my spiritual life.'"

3. Contemplative Practice

Contemplative practice is related but distinct from spiritual direction. While spiritual direction may be part of contemplative practice, my colleagues connected their contemplative practice specifically to personal times of silence, solitude, and prayer. Oliver reflected on the impact that thirty minutes of daily silence had upon him. Mia appreciated the "inner spaciousness" that her contemplative practice opened up for her, which aided her in holding space for the pain of others.

Lena spoke of "embodied spiritual practices," or "embodiment practices," which are a form of contemplative practice that emphasize one's bodily experience. Embodied practices are particularly relevant to processing trauma because trauma lives in our bodies and brains, often not within our conscious awareness. Where trauma disconnects or dissociates us from our bodies, embodied practices help us to come back into connection and attunement. Embodiment includes practices like a body scan (i.e., paying attention to how the parts of one's body feel in a given moment), grounding (i.e., paying attention to one's feet and body grounded on the floor or in a chair), and breath work (e.g., deep breathing, box breathing, or breath prayer).

Tommy recalled a time he was asked what it was like to walk away from "his life's work" at the church he had planted and pastored for decades. "I just kind of blurted out, 'Well if that's my life's work I'd be devastated. But that's not my life's work. My life's work is to understand who I am, to find the real me, and to continue to do the work of living into the self that God made because that's where God is." Tommy had come to understand his vocation through the lens of his contemplative practice rather than primarily through his work.

4. Healing Villages

Rachel shared her experiences going to seminary while being in an abusive marriage and finding friends and allies there who helped her to get out of that violent relationship and find the resources she needed to heal. "They were a healing village for me," she said.

Sophia, a ministry leader and trauma recovery coach, shared a similar sentiment: "It takes a community to [heal] together. It's not just one person. It takes a whole village to be with one another and to just hold each other, to hold each other's hand, to hold space."

My colleagues mentioned different ways that community was a source of healing for them — a healing village. Some spoke about their experiences of healing villages in terms of friendship, others in terms of friendship particularly with those who were different than them, still others in terms of receiving mentoring and coaching. These relationships did not take the form of an official role or capacity, as with therapy or spiritual direction, though certainly they shared similar functions like deep listening and empathetic witnessing.

A Word for White Male Pastors

Good research practice includes naming one's own social location and how it might impact one's research — a concept known as reflexivity. There is no such thing as an objective, detached, unbiased researcher. The presence of the researcher, whether in observation, participation, or listening, invariably affects the results. Part of my social location is my identity as a straight white male. I carry the attending power and privilege of whiteness and maleness and straightness with me into my relationships. I may be reading my social location into the interviews. My colleagues might be responding to me and my social location in their comments. They might have had particularly traumatic experiences with straight white male pastors. Or all of the above.

It's interesting, then, that one of my takeaways from the conversations about personal healing is that white male pastors in particular need to do this healing work — a group that, according to Data USA, comprises more than 60% of all clergy.[1] My colleagues mentioned several reasons for this. First, we straight white males tend to be more resistant to healing work. Ethan observed that in his context they couldn't find many pastors (read: straight white males in the conservative evangelical context to which he was referring) who were interested to do this healing work. Perhaps this is because of the way we are socialized to suppress our feelings, to be aggressive and achievement-oriented, or not to be vulnerable. Or perhaps it just doesn't feel like we have the time and space to fall apart, as it were, with all the responsibilities and expectations we carry as pastors.

Second, we white males are, in fact, wounded. We may not be subject to wounding in the same ways as our siblings at the margins because of our alignment with power structures, but we are wounded nonetheless (though I would venture a guess that many of us may have been wounded in our early, vulnerable years in much the same ways). White males are diminished by patriarchy, Lena asserted, a form of "generational wounding in their families" that is passed down through socialization from fathers to their sons.

Third, if we white males refuse to engage our own healing work, we will perpetuate the harms of white supremacist patriarchy. Lena suggested that if white males approach trauma-informed ministry only as a skillset to acquire, it could become a form of white male saviorism, repeating the same unhealthy patriarchal dynamics of paternalism and domination with new clothing.

Ethan offers strong encouragement for this healing work — to all of us, and particularly for us white male pastors: "The greatest work you'll ever do in your life is nothing you'll ever get a degree for, no one will ever notice it outwardly, but it's the work between you and God that no one will ever see — the mining of your heart, mind, and soul."

| 6 |

Conclusion

I have returned again and again to the words of my mentor and coauthor of my first book, Elaine Heath, for a vision both of where we are headed in the future and what our work is in the present:

> *We are at the forefront of a new reformation, one that is freeing the Christian faith from the sinful structures of patriarchy, racism, classism, many phobias, and exploitive forms of mission and evangelism. The new reformation is all about the emergence of a generous, hospitable, equitable form of Christianity that heals the wounds of the world. I believe much of the work for the church in the years ahead must focus on healing the wounds inflicted by Christendom so that the beauty and inclusive goodness of the gospel can be heard, seen, and experienced.*[1]

Faith leaders in the years ahead must focus on healing the wounds inflicted by Christendom, and as those wounds are healed, a new form of Christianity will emerge that is a healing salve for the world's wounds. The scope and vision is global, but the starting point — one of them at least — is with faith leaders who would seek to help others find healing.

Inspired by this vision, I have sought in this book to explore the question: *how do leaders become trauma-informed agents of healing?* What I learned from my pastoral, therapeutic, and educator colleagues was that this process is built upon three foundations. First, faith leaders have to learn about trauma — a word that literally means wound — both in theory and through experience. Second, faith leaders have to develop the necessary skills, both interpersonal and systemic, in order to offer trauma-responsive spiritual care. And third, perhaps most fundamentally, faith leaders must do their own work, attend to their own interiors and bodies, and pursue their own personal healing. If we fail to process our pain we will inevitably pass it on to those we care for and the cycles of violence and trauma will continue.

God is an empathetic witness to our pain and to the pain of the world.

At the center of the vision above is the healing presence of God. In chapter 1, I referenced Gabor Maté's definition of trauma — "what we hold inside in the absence of an empathetic witness." Trauma — "what we hold inside" — heals in the presence of an empathetic witness who bears witness to the stories of harm, mourns and grieves the injustice with survivors, and stands with them as they put the pieces of their lives back together.

God is an empathetic witness to our pain and to the pain of the world. God suffers with us. God mourns and grieves the injustice we experience. And God walks alongside of us as we put the pieces back together.

The invitation for faith leaders "to focus on healing the wounds inflicted by Christendom," is not an invitation for us to figure out how to heal the world. It is rather an invitation to participate in God's healing work that is already underway. It is an invitation to join God as empathetic witnesses to the pain of others. It is an invitation to allow God to be an empathetic witness to our own pain.

Notes

Chapter 2: Cultivating Trauma Awareness

1. Bessel van der Kolk, *The Body Keeps the Score: Brain, Mind, and Body in the Healing of Trauma* (New York: Penguin Books, 2015), 21.
2. In the foreword to Peter A. Levine's *In an Unspoken Voice: How the Body Releases Trauma and Restores Goodness* (Berkeley, CA: North Atlantic Books, Kindle, loc. 151.

Chapter 5: Pursuing Personal Healing

1. https://datausa.io/profile/soc/clergy, which draws on Census Bureau data, shows that 75.5% of US clergy are white, and 80.5% of US clergy are male.

Chapter 6: The New Reformation

1. Charles Kiser and Elaine A. Heath, *Trauma Informed Evangelism: Cultivating Communities of Wounded Healers* (Grand Rapids: Eerdmans Publishing, 2023), 15.

Recommended Resources

Laura Anderson, *When Religion Hurts You: Healing from Religious Trauma and the Impact of High Control Religion* (Grand Rapids: Brazos Press, 2023).

Chuck DeGroat, *Healing What's Within: Coming Home to Yourself—and to God—When You're Wounded, Weary, and Wandering* (Carol Stream, IL: Tyndale Refresh, 2024).

Robert M. Emerson, Rachel I. Fretz, and Linda L. Shaw, *Writing Ethnographic Fieldnotes*, 2nd ed. (Chicago: University of Chicago Press, 2011).

Judith Herman, *Trauma and Recovery: The Aftermath of Violence — From Domestic Abuse to Political Terror* (New York: Basic Books, 2022).

Aundi Kobler, *Try Softer: A Fresh Approach to Move us out of Anxiety, Stress, and Survival Mode—and into a Life of Connection and Joy* (Carol Stream, IL: Tyndale Refresh, 2020).

Charles Kiser and Elaine A. Heath, *Trauma-Informed Evangelism: Cultivating Communities of Wounded Healers* (Grand Rapids: Eerdmans, 2023).

Bessel van der Kolk, *The Body Keeps the Score: Brain, Mind, and Body in the Healing of Trauma* (New York: Penguin Books, 2015).

Diane Langberg, *Redeeming Power: Understanding Authority and Abuse in the Church* (Grand Rapids: Brazos Press, 2020).

Peter Levine, *In an Unspoken Voice: How the Body Releases Trauma and Restores Goodness* (Berkeley: North Atlantic Books, 2010).

Hillary McBride, *The Wisdom of the Body: Finding Healing, Wholeness, and Connection through Embodied Living* (Grand Rapids: Brazos Press, 2021).

Janyne McConnaughey, *Trauma in the Pews: The Impact on Faith and Spiritual Practices* (Glendora, CA: Berry Powell Press, 2022).

Resmaa Menakem, *My Grandmother's Hands: Racialized Trauma and the Pathway to Mending Our Hearts and Bodies* (Las Vegas: Central Recovery Press, 2017).

Mallory Wyckoff, *God Is* (Grand Rapids: Eerdmans, 2022).

Instagram Accounts

- Broken to Beloved
- Chuck DeGroat
- Dan Coke
- David Ruybalid
- DrJanyneMc
- Dr. Laura Anderson
- Jenai Auman
- Kat Wilkins Counseling
- TheHealingCollective.Space

Charles Kiser is a pastor, theologian, author, coach, and trainer. He is the coauthor with Elaine Heath of *Trauma-Informed Evangelism: Cultivating Communities of Wounded Healers,* which emerged out of his sixteen-year pastoral work among spiritually traumatized folks in Dallas, Texas. He is the Cofounder and Codirector of The Healing Collective (www.thehealingcollective.space), a ministry that creates spaces for healing religious trauma. Kiser is also the Regional Area Developer for the Dallas-Fort Worth area of the Post-Evangelical Collective (www.postevangelicalcollective.org), an organization that seeks to connect and resource post-evangelical leaders and cultivate new post-evangelical churches that function as healing communities. Kiser holds a doctorate in contextual theology and his work focuses on the intersection of post-colonial mission, contemplative spirituality, and trauma healing. He writes about all of this at www.empatheticwitness.substack.com. Kiser lives in the Dallas area with his wife, their three kids, and their frenetic Boston Terrier, Gus.

www.ingramcontent.com/pod-product-compliance
Lightning Source LLC
LaVergne TN
LVHW101617210926
848480LV00009B/787
* 9 7 9 8 3 4 9 2 7 1 2 2 9 *